TEXAS TEST PREP

Reading Workbook

STAAR Reading

Grade 7

ISBN 978-1463524593

CONTENTS

INTRODUCTION
For Parents, Teachers, and Tutors

About the Book

The STAAR Reading test taken by all Texas students contains reading passages followed by reading comprehension questions. This reading workbook contains passages and question sets similar to those on the STAAR reading tests, but much shorter. The questions are just like those found on the STAAR tests and cover all the same skills.

By having ongoing test practice with short passages and small question sets, students will gradually develop the reading skills that all Texas students need. This book is designed for students to have ongoing test prep practice as part of their homework routine. Without the stress of long complex passages and long question sets, students can develop the reading skills needed while gaining confidence and becoming familiar with answering reading comprehension questions.

The practice sets are divided into 8 sets of 5 passages each. The Score Tracker in the back of the book can be used to record student progress. As the student completes each set, tally the scores. As the student progresses through the sets, test scores will continue to improve as the students develops reading skills and gains confidence.

STAAR Reading Skills

The STAAR reading test given by the state of Texas tests a specific set of skills. The full answer key at the end of the book identifies what skill each question is testing.

There are also key reading skills that students will need to understand to master the STAAR reading test. The answer key includes additional information on these key skills so you can help the student gain understanding.

Reading Workbook

STAAR Reading

Set 1

Instructions

Read each passage. Each passage is followed by three questions.

Read each question carefully. Then select the best answer. Fill in the circle for the correct answer.

Flying High

My family and I live near the airport. Some people think that's a bad thing, but I think it's great. I've always loved watching the airplanes fly way up high. They soar overhead like giant metallic birds.

My mom and dad always complain about the noise, especially late at night. But not me! I love everything about airplanes. When I grow up and move into my own place, I hope it's near an airport too. Maybe I'll even fly an airplane one day. That would be like a dream come true.

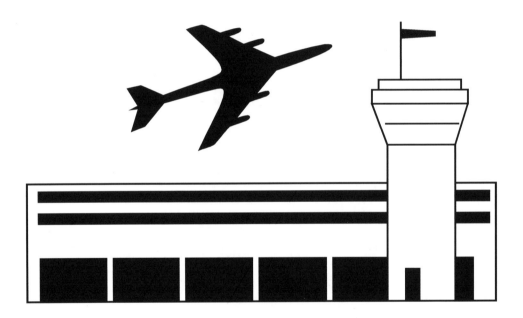

1   Which two words from the passage have about the same meaning?

    Ⓐ   *airplanes, airport*

    Ⓑ   *bad, great*

    Ⓒ   *fly, soar*

    Ⓓ   *noise, dream*

2   How is the narrator similar to his parents?

    Ⓐ   He likes watching the airplanes.

    Ⓑ   He finds the sound of the airplanes annoying.

    Ⓒ   He wants to fly an airplane some day.

    Ⓓ   He lives near the airport.

3   When do the narrator's parents find the planes most annoying?

    Ⓐ   Early in the morning

    Ⓑ   In the afternoon

    Ⓒ   Around dinner time

    Ⓓ   Late at night

King of the Jungle

The lion is a member of the family Felidae and one of the four big cats of the Panthera genus. Exceptionally large male lions can weigh over 550 pounds, making them the second largest living cat after the tiger.

Lions can be found in Africa and in northwest India. In the wild, lions usually live for between 10 and 14 years. Lions in captivity have been known to live for over 20 years. The lion is a vulnerable species. It has seen a steady population decline over the last two decades.

1   Read this sentence from the passage.

> **It has seen a steady population decline over the last two decades.**

Which word means the opposite of <u>steady</u>?

Ⓐ   Worrying

Ⓑ   Rapid

Ⓒ   Regular

Ⓓ   Gradual

2   What is the overall tone of the passage?

Ⓐ   Serious

Ⓑ   Humorous

Ⓒ   Regretful

Ⓓ   Informal

3   Which conclusion is best supported by the passage?

Ⓐ   There are more lions in captivity than in the wild.

Ⓑ   Lions tend to live longer in captivity than in the wild.

Ⓒ   Lions living in captivity lose some of their key skills.

Ⓓ   Breeding lions in captivity is one way they can be saved.

Gone Fishing

One day Tony and Damien decided to go fishing. They really enjoyed going fishing and were really excited. They got their fishing gear ready at Damien's house. They stopped by the local store to buy some bait and some snacks. On their way to the beach, they talked about all the fish they were going to catch.

Tony and Damien arrived at the beach and both cast out their fishing lines. They both waited anxiously for their first catch. There were a few nibbles as the hours went by, but no fish. Finally, after a long day and lots of laughs, Tony let out a sigh. It was time to go home. Tony and Damien didn't catch any fish that day, but at least they had fun.

1 Read this sentence from the passage.

> **Finally, after a long day and lots of laughs, Tony let out a sigh.**

Tony most likely sighs because he is –

Ⓐ tired

Ⓑ excited

Ⓒ angry

Ⓓ hot

2 What is the main setting of the passage?

Ⓐ A beach

Ⓑ Tony's house

Ⓒ A local store

Ⓓ A river

3 The main theme of the passage is about –

Ⓐ being organized

Ⓑ making the most of things

Ⓒ taking your time

Ⓓ never giving up

The Capybara

There are approximately 2,200 species of rodents. Among the largest common rodents are beavers and chipmunks. However, most people associate the term rodent with rats or mice.

The largest rodent is the giant rat, or capybara. It can be found living in many countries in South America. The capybara can grow up to 4 feet long and can weigh anywhere between 75 and 150 pounds. They are mainly found near bodies of water, including in swamps. Capybaras are even found in the wetlands of Florida. Capybaras are herbivores and feed on plants, bark, and nuts.

1   Complete the web below using information from the passage.

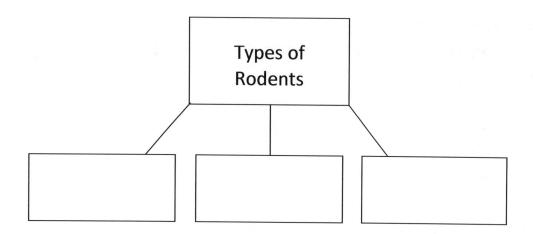

Types of Rodents

2   In the first paragraph, which word could best be used in place of <u>associate</u>?

    Ⓐ   Understand

    Ⓑ   Organize

    Ⓒ   Connect

    Ⓓ   Imagine

3   The author probably wrote the passage mainly to –

    Ⓐ   describe animals common to Florida

    Ⓑ   compare and contrast different rodents

    Ⓒ   give facts about one species of rodent

    Ⓓ   convince readers that rodents are not pests

The Dentist

Dear Aunt Sienna,

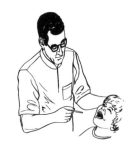

Today I went to the dentist and had some fillings put in. It wasn't the worst thing in the world. I wasn't looking forward to it, but it actually didn't take very long and didn't hurt at all! I could definitely think of better things to do though.

When I got home, my mouth felt all weird and tingly. I spent most of the afternoon just reading through comic books and lying in bed. Mom told me that she had fillings put in when she was around my age. I think maybe I should be eating less candy and brushing more!

Bye for now,

Becky

1   Read this sentence from the passage.

When I got home, my mouth felt all weird and tingly.

Which word means about the same as <u>weird</u>?

Ⓐ   Stinging

Ⓑ   Sore

Ⓒ   Warm

Ⓓ   Strange

2   How did Becky most likely feel just before getting the fillings in?

Ⓐ   Relieved

Ⓑ   Uneasy

Ⓒ   Thrilled

Ⓓ   Confident

3   What can the reader tell because the passage has a first person point of view?

Ⓐ   Why Becky went to the dentist

Ⓑ   How Becky felt about going to the dentist

Ⓒ   What Becky did after leaving the dentist

Ⓓ   How long Becky was at the dentist for

Reading Workbook

STAAR Reading

Set 2

Instructions

Read each passage. Each passage is followed by three questions.

Read each question carefully. Then select the best answer. Fill in the circle for the correct answer.

A Quiet Night

Gloria lit the candle on her windowsill and sat on her bed dressed in her white nightgown. She snuggled up under the covers and propped a thick pillow up against the nightstand. She opened up her book and began to read. She turned page after page as the candle slowly burned down. The candle flickered slightly. Gloria looked over at her clock.

"Ah, bed time," Gloria said, as the hands struck nine o'clock.

She put her book down on her bedside table, blew out the candle, and went to sleep.

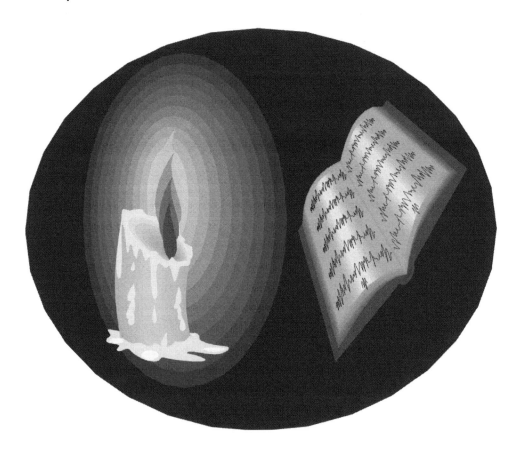

1 Read this sentence from the passage.

> **She snuggled up under the covers and propped a thick pillow up against the nightstand.**

Which word from the sentence suggests that Gloria was comfortable?

Ⓐ *snuggled*

Ⓑ *propped*

Ⓒ *against*

Ⓓ *nightstand*

2 Which word best describes the mood of the passage?

Ⓐ Mysterious

Ⓑ Joyful

Ⓒ Peaceful

Ⓓ Gloomy

3 Which detail in the passage is used to represent time passing?

Ⓐ Gloria lighting the candle

Ⓑ The candle burning down

Ⓒ The candle flickering

Ⓓ Gloria blowing out the candle

Hillary Clinton

Hillary Clinton was born on October 26, 1947. She was the First Lady of the United States from 1993 to 2001, as the wife of President Bill Clinton. In 2001, she became a Senator for the state of New York. She remained in this role until 2009. In January of 2009, she became the 67th United States Secretary of State, serving under President Barack Obama. Just prior to this, Clinton was also considered as a candidate to run for president.

1   Read this sentence from the passage.

> **In January of 2009, she became the 67th United States Secretary of State, serving under President Barack Obama.**

Which meaning of the word <u>serving</u> is used in the sentence?

Ⓐ   Providing customers with goods

Ⓑ   Being in the armed services

Ⓒ   Giving people food or drink

Ⓓ   Working for somebody

2   Where would this passage most likely be found?

Ⓐ   In an encyclopedia

Ⓑ   In a travel guide

Ⓒ   In a newspaper

Ⓓ   In a book of short stories

3   What was Hillary Clinton's first role in politics?

Ⓐ   Senator for New York

Ⓑ   First Lady

Ⓒ   Secretary of State

Ⓓ   Candidate for president

I Have a Dream

Martin Luther King, Jr. was born in 1929. He is one of the most famous people in history to be associated with the civil rights movement. At age 35, King became the youngest person to ever receive a Nobel Peace Prize. He received it for his tireless work to end racial inequality.

He is probably best known for his "I Have a Dream" speech. He delivered this famous speech after leading the 1963 March on Washington. Martin Luther King is honored with his own holiday. The third Monday of January every year is Martin Luther King, Jr. Day.

1   Read this sentence from the passage.

He received it for his tireless work to end racial inequality.

Which word means about the same as <u>tireless</u>?

Ⓐ   Difficult

Ⓑ   Effective

Ⓒ   Essential

Ⓓ   Determined

2   What type of passage is "I Have a Dream"?

Ⓐ   Biography

Ⓑ   Short story

Ⓒ   Autobiography

Ⓓ   News article

3   Which sentence from the passage best supports the idea that the work of Martin Luther King, Jr. is appreciated?

Ⓐ   *Martin Luther King, Jr. was born in 1929.*

Ⓑ   *He is probably best known for his "I Have a Dream" speech.*

Ⓒ   *He delivered this famous speech after leading the 1963 March on Washington.*

Ⓓ   *Martin Luther King is honored with his own holiday.*

Artistic Creativity

Every day I enjoy being creative. Some days you will find me painting a portrait. Other days I may be writing a short fiction novel. I even find enjoyment out of sculpting something strange and bizarre into life.

Being artistic is important to me. Every artistic work is a chance to show my own unique style and create something that only I could have created. I fancy myself as quite the individual!

1 Read this sentence from the passage.

> **I even find enjoyment out of sculpting something strange and bizarre into life.**

Which word means the opposite of <u>bizarre</u>?

- Ⓐ Ordinary
- Ⓑ Weird
- Ⓒ Rare
- Ⓓ Special

2 Which creative activity is NOT described in the passage?

- Ⓐ Writing
- Ⓑ Sculpting
- Ⓒ Dancing
- Ⓓ Painting

3 What is the point of view in the passage?

- Ⓐ First person
- Ⓑ Second person
- Ⓒ Third person limited
- Ⓓ Third person omniscient

What Caterpillars Do

What, oh what do caterpillars do?
They don't do much but chew and chew.
What, oh what do caterpillars know?
They don't know much but how to grow.

They can't watch TV, go fishing, or cry,
But they can turn into a butterfly.
That is more than I can do,
No matter how much I chew, chew, chew.

1   Which word best describes the mood of the poem?

    Ⓐ   Gloomy

    Ⓑ   Mysterious

    Ⓒ   Frustrating

    Ⓓ   Cheerful

2   Which literary device is used in the poem?

    Ⓐ   Flashback

    Ⓑ   Repetition

    Ⓒ   Similes

    Ⓓ   Personification

3   What is the rhyme pattern of each stanza of the poem?

    Ⓐ   Every line rhymes.

    Ⓑ   The second and fourth lines rhyme.

    Ⓒ   The first and last lines rhyme.

    Ⓓ   There are two sets of rhyming lines.

Reading Workbook

STAAR Reading

Set 3

Instructions

Read each passage. Each passage is followed by three questions.

Read each question carefully. Then select the best answer. Fill in the circle for the correct answer.

Be Prepared

The Scouts is a worldwide youth movement aimed at supporting the physical and mental development of young males. The Scouts was started in 1907 by Robert Baden-Powell, who was a Lieutenant General in the British Army.

During the 1900s, the movement grew to include three different age groups of boys. The Cub Scouts is for boys aged from 7 to 11. The Scouts is for boys aged 11 to 18. The Rover Scouts is for boys aged over 18. In 1910, a similar organization was created for girls. It is known as the Girl Guides. The motto of the Scouts is "Be Prepared."

1   Complete the table below using information from the passage.

Age Groups for Boys

Group	Age
Cub Scouts	7 to 11

2   If the author added another paragraph to the passage, what would it be most likely to describe?

Ⓐ   What Robert Baden-Powell's childhood was like

Ⓑ   Who started the Girl Guides

Ⓒ   What activities the Scouts do

Ⓓ   How to join the Scouts

3   Which word could best be used in place of <u>worldwide</u> in the first sentence?

Ⓐ   Noteworthy

Ⓑ   Relevant

Ⓒ   International

Ⓓ   Established

Breaking In

Today, Apple is a success in the personal computer market. It offers a range of effective and attractive products. But it wasn't always that way. Apple had to struggle to break into the market.

At the time, IBM was the leader in the market. Then Apple introduced the iMac G3 in 1998. The iMac G3 was one of the first commercial successes for Apple. Previous to the iMac, Apple saw only limited success with its earlier desktop models.

The iMac G3 came after new Apple CEO Steve Jobs decided to trim Apple's product line. He decided to relaunch with a focus on simplicity. It was a bold move and an effective one. The striking design of the iMac was just one of the reasons it was special.

1   Read this sentence from the passage.

> **The iMac G3 came after new Apple CEO Steve Jobs decided to trim Apple's product line.**

The word <u>trim</u> is used to show that Steve Jobs –

Ⓐ   made each product smaller

Ⓑ   reduced the number of products

Ⓒ   decreased the weight of the products

Ⓓ   made the products look more attractive

2   The author probably wrote this passage to –

Ⓐ   encourage people to buy Apple products

Ⓑ   describe a turning point for a company

Ⓒ   analyze the sales techniques of a computer company

Ⓓ   tell about the life of Steve Jobs

3   Which sentence from the passage is a fact?

Ⓐ   *It offers a range of effective and attractive products.*

Ⓑ   *Then Apple introduced the iMac G3 in 1998.*

Ⓒ   *It was a bold move and an effective one.*

Ⓓ   *The striking design of the iMac was just one of the reasons it was special.*

Hide and Seek

Jeremy pulled the door to his closet shut slowly.

"Ready or not, here I come!" Vanessa yelled from the kitchen.

Jeremy snickered a little. He knew Vanessa would never find him in his closet. Vanessa could be heard ruffling through different places for a short while before everything went quiet. Jeremy leaned over and peeked out the door.

"Ahhhhh!" Jeremy let out a yell like he had just seen a ghost.

Vanessa's face was right in front of the closet door staring back at him.

"Found you," Vanessa giggled and ran off.

1   Read this sentence from the passage.

       Jeremy snickered a little.

    Which word means about the same as <u>snickered</u>?

    Ⓐ   Laughed

    Ⓑ   Sighed

    Ⓒ   Chatted

    Ⓓ   Coughed

2   Which sentence from the passage contains a simile?

    Ⓐ   *Jeremy pulled the door to his closet shut slowly.*

    Ⓑ   *He knew Vanessa would never find him in his closet.*

    Ⓒ   *Jeremy leaned over and peeked out the door.*

    Ⓓ   *Jeremy let out a yell like he had just seen a ghost.*

3   Why does Jeremy most likely close the closet door slowly?

    Ⓐ   So he does not get stuck in the closet

    Ⓑ   So he can still see out of the closet

    Ⓒ   So Vanessa does not hear him

    Ⓓ   So he does not scare Vanessa

Cartoons

Every morning before school, I love to watch cartoons. People say I'm getting too old for cartoons, but I just think that cartoons are funny. My big sister Annie always reminds me that I'm not a kid anymore. But I think anyone can watch cartoons, not just kids.

The jokes are what I like the best. Plus I love watching something that isn't serious at all. You can just let go and enjoy the show! I don't think I'll ever stop watching cartoons, even if other people think I'm too old for them.

1 Read this sentence from the passage.

You can just let go and enjoy the show!

What does the phrase "let go" refer to?

Ⓐ Sitting

Ⓑ Relaxing

Ⓒ Waiting

Ⓓ Stopping

2 Which sentence from the passage best shows the main idea?

Ⓐ *My big sister Annie always reminds me that I'm not a kid anymore.*

Ⓑ *The jokes are what I like the best.*

Ⓒ *Plus I love watching something that isn't serious at all.*

Ⓓ *I don't think I'll ever stop watching cartoons, even if other people think I'm too old for them.*

3 What is the second paragraph mostly about?

Ⓐ Why the narrator likes cartoons

Ⓑ How the narrator is too old for cartoons

Ⓒ When the narrator likes to watch cartoons

Ⓓ What other people think of cartoons

Defeat at Waterloo

Napoleon Bonaparte was a legendary military leader during the late stages of the French Revolution. He was leader of the French Army and led the French to wins in many major battles. He later became Emperor of France and continued to lead the French through many successful battles. For over ten years, the French seemed unbeatable.

The Imperial French Army was finally defeated in 1815 at the Battle of Waterloo. The French Army was again led by Napoleon, but this time he was on the losing side. An enormous coalition of European forces battled against the French and won.

The events of Napoleon's life fired the imagination of great writers and filmmakers. Their works have continued to foster the legend of Napoleon.

1   Read this sentence from the passage.

> **The events of Napoleon's life fired the imagination of great writers and filmmakers.**

The word <u>fired</u> suggests that the writers and filmmakers were —

Ⓐ   angered by Napoleon

Ⓑ   paid well for their work

Ⓒ   forced to write about Napoleon

Ⓓ   inspired by Napoleon

2   Which word would the author most likely use to describe Napoleon as a military leader?

Ⓐ   Imaginative

Ⓑ   Impressive

Ⓒ   Stubborn

Ⓓ   Average

3   What is the second paragraph mainly about?

Ⓐ   Napoleon's success as a leader

Ⓑ   Napoleon's eventual downfall

Ⓒ   The importance of Napoleon to France

Ⓓ   How Napoleon is remembered today

Reading Workbook

STAAR Reading

Set 4

Instructions

Read each passage. Each passage is followed by three questions.

Read each question carefully. Then select the best answer. Fill in the circle for the correct answer.

Flying Scavengers

The Andean Condor is a species of South American bird in the vulture family. It can be found in the Andes mountain range and the Pacific coasts of western South America. The Andean Condor is the largest flying land bird in the Western Hemisphere. Unlike most birds of prey, the male Andean Condor is larger than the female.

1   In what family is the Andean Condor?

     Ⓐ   Hawk

     Ⓑ   Eagle

     Ⓒ   Toucan

     Ⓓ   Vulture

2   Where would this passage most likely be found?

     Ⓐ   In a book of poems

     Ⓑ   In an encyclopedia

     Ⓒ   In a newspaper

     Ⓓ   In a book of short stories

3   What is the main purpose of the passage?

     Ⓐ   To instruct

     Ⓑ   To entertain

     Ⓒ   To persuade

     Ⓓ   To inform

Danny's Homework

Danny was sitting down on the rug and tapping away at the keys on his laptop. He was working on his homework, when all of a sudden his laptop turned off.

"No!" he panicked, pressing the power button repeatedly. He stood up and ran over to his desk with his laptop. Plugging it into the charger, he waited as the laptop booted up again.

"Ding!" said the laptop excitedly as it started up. Danny let out a huge sigh when he saw that his homework file had automatically saved.

"That was a close one," he said.

1   Read this sentence from the passage.

"Ding!" said the laptop excitedly as it started up.

Which literary device does the author use in this sentence?

Ⓐ   Simile

Ⓑ   Alliteration

Ⓒ   Imagery

Ⓓ   Personification

2   Why did the laptop most likely shut down?

Ⓐ   It had a fault.

Ⓑ   It ran out of power.

Ⓒ   Danny knocked it over.

Ⓓ   Danny shut the lid.

3   Which word best describes how Danny feels when he sees that his homework has saved?

Ⓐ   Relieved

Ⓑ   Alarmed

Ⓒ   Stressed

Ⓓ   Excited

The Evil Candide

The princess wished the prince good morrow and went to bed. During the night, the princess was stolen by an evil sorcerer named Candide. Candide was always envious of the prince. He wanted the princess all to himself.

When the prince awoke the next morning to find the princess missing, he knew who had taken her right away. The prince dressed in his finest armor, took up his sword, and galloped off towards Candide's lair to save the princess.

1   Read this sentence from the passage.

Candide was always envious of the prince.

Which word means about the same as <u>envious</u>?

Ⓐ   Afraid

Ⓑ   Impressed

Ⓒ   Annoyed

Ⓓ   Jealous

2   Which words used in the passage suggest that the story takes place a long time ago?

Ⓐ   *good morrow*

Ⓑ   *all to himself*

Ⓒ   *the next morning*

Ⓓ   *galloped off*

3   What will most likely happen next in the passage?

Ⓐ   The princess will run away.

Ⓑ   The prince will save the princess.

Ⓒ   Candide will take the princess home.

Ⓓ   The prince will seek out a new princess.

Radiohead

Radiohead are an alternative rock band from Oxfordshire in England. They are a five piece band that first formed in 1985. They released their first single, titled "Creep," in 1992. The song was initially unsuccessful. However, it became a hit after the release of their debut album, titled *Pablo Honey*, in 1993. Radiohead's first six albums had sold more than 25 million copies by 2007.

1 Read this sentence from the passage.

> **Radiohead's first six albums had sold more than 25 million copies by 2007.**

Why does the author most likely include this sentence?

Ⓐ To show that Radiohead stayed together a long time

Ⓑ To show the reader that Radiohead achieved success

Ⓒ To show that Radiohead's first single was a hit

Ⓓ To show the reader the style of Radiohead's music

2 How is the passage mainly organized?

Ⓐ A solution to a problem is described.

Ⓑ Events are described in the order they occurred.

Ⓒ Facts are given to support an argument.

Ⓓ An event in the past is compared to an event today.

3 What is the main purpose of the passage?

Ⓐ To give details about a successful band

Ⓑ To encourage people to listen to music

Ⓒ To argue that bands are better than solo artists

Ⓓ To explain why a band was popular

Belarus

Belarus is a landlocked country in Eastern Europe. The capital of Belarus is Minsk. Minsk has an estimated population of just over two million. Around forty percent of the country is forested. This makes agriculture one of Belarus' strongest industries. Following the collapse of the Soviet Union, Belarus declared its independence in 1991. Belarus has two official languages: Belarusian and Russian.

1   Which sentence from the passage is supported by the map?

    Ⓐ   *Belarus is a landlocked country in Eastern Europe.*

    Ⓑ   *Minsk has an estimated population of just over two million.*

    Ⓒ   *Around forty percent of the country is forested.*

    Ⓓ   *Belarus has two official languages: Belarusian and Russian.*

2   Which of the following would NOT be found in Belarus?

    Ⓐ   Forest

    Ⓑ   Ocean

    Ⓒ   River

    Ⓓ   Lake

3   Where would this passage most likely be found?

    Ⓐ   In a science magazine

    Ⓑ   In a book of short stories

    Ⓒ   In an encyclopedia

    Ⓓ   In a travel guide

Reading Workbook

STAAR Reading

Set 5

Instructions

Read each passage. Each passage is followed by three questions.

Read each question carefully. Then select the best answer. Fill in the circle for the correct answer.

The Dog and the River

A dog was crossing a river by walking across a log. He had a small but juicy piece of meat in his mouth. He saw his own reflection and mistook it for another dog with a piece of meat double the size of his own. He immediately dropped his own piece of meat and attacked the other dog to get the larger piece. His paw struck at his reflection, only to hit the water below. His own piece of meat fell off into the river and the dog was left with nothing.

1   What type of passage is "The Dog and the River"?

    Ⓐ   Realistic fiction

    Ⓑ   Biography

    Ⓒ   Science fiction

    Ⓓ   Fable

2   What is the main lesson the dog learns in the passage?

    Ⓐ   Bigger is usually better.

    Ⓑ   Be thankful for what you have.

    Ⓒ   Be careful when crossing rivers.

    Ⓓ   Fighting does not achieve anything.

3   Which of the following is the best summary of the passage?

    Ⓐ   A dog with a small piece of meat thinks his reflection is a dog with a large piece of meat. He tries to get the large piece and ends up with no meat.

    Ⓑ   A dog sees another dog with a better piece of meat. He drops his own piece. He loses the fight with the other dog.

    Ⓒ   A dog thinks he sees a dog with a larger piece of meat. He drops his own meat. Then he realizes that the other piece of meat is not real. He regrets the decision that he made.

    Ⓓ   A dog is crossing a river with a small piece of meat. He drops the meat into the river. He is unable to get it back.

Bananas

April 14

Dear Diary,

Today Dad told me that I've been opening a banana wrong all of my life. I thought he was messing with me!

Then Dad took me to the zoo and showed me how a monkey opens a banana. They don't do it from the stem end. They grab the tip, pinch it, and peel one side down, and then peel the other side. It's so easy. I have to admit I was impressed.

Well, now I know I've been opening a banana wrong all of my life. I don't know what is worse – having to admit that Dad was right or having to admit that a monkey is smarter than me!

Bye for now,

Harmanie xo

1   Read this sentence from the passage.

I thought he was messing with me!

What does this sentence mean?

Ⓐ   I thought he was wrong.

Ⓑ   I thought he was teasing me.

Ⓒ   I thought he was cleaning.

Ⓓ   I thought he was mad at me.

2   What does a monkey do first when peeling a banana?

Ⓐ   Pinches the tip of the banana

Ⓑ   Grabs the tip of the banana

Ⓒ   Peels one side of the banana down

Ⓓ   Squeezes the stem of the banana

3   How does Harmanie most likely feel when she sees how monkeys eat bananas?

Ⓐ   Annoyed

Ⓑ   Puzzled

Ⓒ   Surprised

Ⓓ   Unimpressed

Brain in a Bottle

Did you know that the remains of Einstein's brain are stored at Princeton Hospital in New Jersey? Dr. Thomas Harvey was the doctor who had to conduct the initial autopsy on Einstein in 1955. Harvey removed Einstein's brain without permission from Einstein's family. He carefully sliced it into sections to keep for research. There are now at least three published papers relating to the study of Einstein's brain.

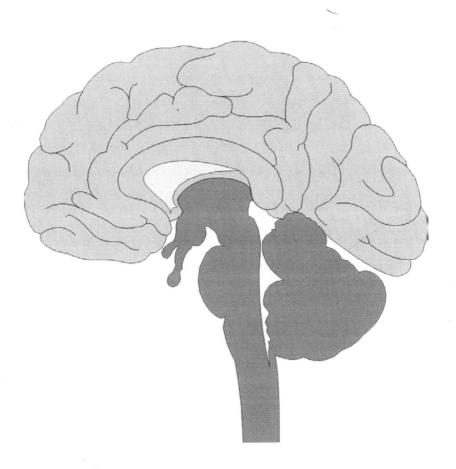

1   Read this sentence from the passage.

> **Dr. Thomas Harvey was the doctor who had to conduct the initial autopsy on Einstein in 1955.**

Which meaning of the word <u>conduct</u> is used in the sentence?

Ⓐ   To transmit heat energy

Ⓑ   To behave in a certain way

Ⓒ   To lead a vocal group

Ⓓ   To carry out

2   Why does the author begin the passage with a question?

Ⓐ   To get readers interested in the topic of the passage

Ⓑ   To show that Dr. Thomas Harvey did the wrong thing

Ⓒ   To suggest that readers should research the topic

Ⓓ   To explain how scientists learn by asking questions

3   What is the passage mainly about?

Ⓐ   How Einstein's brain was kept

Ⓑ   How scientists conduct research

Ⓒ   Why doctors should follow rules

Ⓓ   Why Einstein was a genius

Antique Map

It's really easy and fun to make a map look likes it's an old antique. You'll need to print out a map or get permission to use an old map that is no longer needed. You'll also need to make some strong black tea (make sure you let it cool down) and a spray bottle to put the tea in.

Step 1: Place the map on a clean flat surface that will be easy to clean afterwards.

Step 2: Soak the entire map by spraying it evenly with black tea.

Step 3: Gently lift the map after it is sprayed to make sure it does not stick to the flat surface.

Step 4: Allow the map to dry and repeat steps 1 to 3 until you achieve the desired effect.

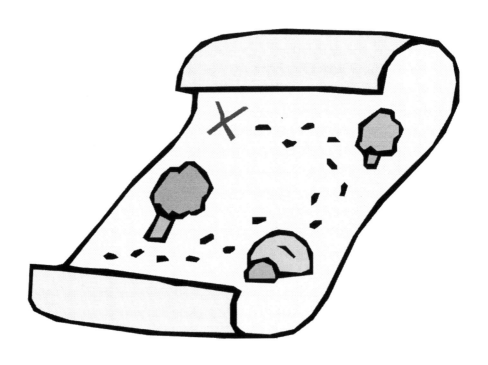

1 What is the main purpose of the first sentence of the passage?

Ⓐ To show the items needed for the project

Ⓑ To explain what makes maps look older

Ⓒ To encourage people to want to complete the project

Ⓓ To show that the author has experience with the project

2 In which step is the black tea first needed?

Ⓐ Step 1

Ⓑ Step 2

Ⓒ Step 3

Ⓓ Step 4

3 What is the most likely reason it is important to let the black tea cool down?

Ⓐ So the map does not get ruined

Ⓑ So the map changes color

Ⓒ So the tea cannot be consumed

Ⓓ So the tea does not burn anyone

A Special Student

June enjoyed being in school. She enjoyed watching the children play and sometimes sharing their lunches. June enjoyed seeing her friends play skip rope and liked having a nap in the afternoons. June sometimes got to enjoy eating the grass on the football field. June wasn't any ordinary student. June was the school mascot.

June was a cow. Every week, June would enjoy having a class of children milk her. Then she would be let out into the paddock for a graze. What June liked best of all, is when the children petted her. There were always plenty of children happy to pat her, so June was a very happy school mascot. The children loved June just as much as she loved them. They enjoyed spending time with her and looking after her.

1   What is the point of view in the passage?

    Ⓐ   First person

    Ⓑ   Second person

    Ⓒ   Third person limited

    Ⓓ   Third person omniscient

2   What happens right after June is milked?

    Ⓐ   The children pat her.

    Ⓑ   She has a nap.

    Ⓒ   She is let out to graze.

    Ⓓ   She is given a bath.

3   What is the first clue in the passage that June is a cow?

    Ⓐ   She watches the children play.

    Ⓑ   She shares the student's lunches.

    Ⓒ   She has a nap in the afternoon.

    Ⓓ   She eats the grass on the football field.

Reading Workbook

STAAR Reading

Set 6

Instructions

Read each passage. Each passage is followed by three questions.

Read each question carefully. Then select the best answer. Fill in the circle for the correct answer.

Photosynthesis

The process of turning light energy into chemical energy is called photosynthesis. The process of photosynthesis is how plants get their energy.

Plant leaves and stems have a high amount of a green pigment named chlorophyll contained in them. Light energy from the Sun is absorbed by the chlorophyll. This energy is used to power a reaction between water and carbon dioxide. This reaction produces glucose and oxygen. The plant stores the glucose and uses it for energy. The oxygen is released into the air.

1   Which two words from the passage have the opposite meaning?

    Ⓐ   *light, chemical*

    Ⓑ   *leaves, stems*

    Ⓒ   *absorbed, released*

    Ⓓ   *energy, power*

2   What is the main purpose of the passage?

    Ⓐ   To instruct

    Ⓑ   To entertain

    Ⓒ   To persuade

    Ⓓ   To inform

3   According to the passage, what does the photosynthesis reaction produce?

    Ⓐ   Water

    Ⓑ   Carbon dioxide

    Ⓒ   Glucose

    Ⓓ   Light energy

The Little Things

Every morning when Patrick woke up he would throw up his arms, let out a yawn, and jump out of bed.

"Up and at 'em," he'd always bellow loudly.

Patrick had his breakfast and then got dressed in his overalls. He strolled out to his garden to tend to his vibrant flowers and gourmet vegetable patch. Every afternoon, he would bring in new flowers for his wife and some fresh vegetables for dinner.

"It's the little things that make life great," Patrick would always say.

1 Which phrase from the passage creates a mood of calm?

    Ⓐ   *throw up his arms*

    Ⓑ   *always bellow loudly*

    Ⓒ   *dressed in his overalls*

    Ⓓ   *strolled out to his garden*

2 Patrick would most likely describe his life as –

    Ⓐ   difficult and exhausting

    Ⓑ   exciting and carefree

    Ⓒ   dull and disappointing

    Ⓓ   simple but rewarding

3 What is the main theme of the passage about?

    Ⓐ   Enjoying what you have

    Ⓑ   Growing your own food

    Ⓒ   Having a daily routine

    Ⓓ   Forgetting your troubles

Sweet Tooth

Did you know that people originally used to chew sugarcane raw? Sugar has been produced since ancient times and originated in India. However, sugar wasn't always so plentiful and cheap. In the early days, honey was used more often than sugar for sweetening food and beverages. Sugar was also one of the first ingredients used, as it is today, to mask the bitter taste of medicine.

1 Read this sentence from the passage.

> **Sugar was also one of the first ingredients used, as it is today, to mask the bitter taste of medicine.**

Which word could best be used in place of <u>mask</u>?

Ⓐ   Hide

Ⓑ   Sweeten

Ⓒ   Improve

Ⓓ   Destroy

2 Why does the author begin the passage with a question?

Ⓐ   To get readers interested in the topic of the passage

Ⓑ   To show that things have changed since ancient times

Ⓒ   To suggest that readers should research the topic

Ⓓ   To indicate that the information may be incorrect

3 What is the most likely reason honey was used instead of sugar in ancient times?

Ⓐ   Honey tasted sweeter than sugar.

Ⓑ   Honey kept fresh longer than sugar.

Ⓒ   Honey was cheaper than sugar.

Ⓓ   Honey had more uses than sugar.

The Stanley Cup

The Stanley Cup is the most appreciated ice hockey trophy in the world. It is awarded every year to the winner of the National Hockey League (NHL) championships.

Unlike most other sports, a new Stanley Cup is not made each year. The winning team keeps it until new champions are crowned. This makes players appreciate the award even more.

The Stanley Cup is the oldest professional sports trophy in North America. It was donated by the Governor General of Canada Lord Stanley of Preston in 1892.

1 In the first sentence, which word could best be used in place of appreciated?

    Ⓐ   Valued

    Ⓑ   Awarded

    Ⓒ   Ancient

    Ⓓ   Curious

2 Why is the last paragraph important to the passage?

    Ⓐ   It shows that ice hockey has been played for a long time.

    Ⓑ   It shows that ice hockey is a national sport.

    Ⓒ   It shows the long history of the trophy.

    Ⓓ   It shows that the trophy is most important to Canadians.

3 Which sentence from the passage is an opinion?

    Ⓐ   *It is awarded every year to the winner of the National Hockey League (NHL) championships.*

    Ⓑ   *This makes players appreciate the award even more.*

    Ⓒ   *The Stanley Cup is the oldest professional sports trophy in North America.*

    Ⓓ   *It was donated by the Governor General of Canada Lord Stanley of Preston in 1892.*

Snowed In

"HQ, this is Nord, do you copy?" Dr. Nord spoke
into the microphone.

He tapped away at various buttons and waited a
few moments.

"Guess I'm stuck here for another day," Nord said
as he hung his head.

Two days ago, a snow storm had hit the research bunker he was
working in. All communications had been lost. Dr. Nord wasn't worried
though. He knew someone would come looking for him.

1   Read this sentence from the passage.

> **"Guess I'm stuck here for another day," Nord said as he hung his head.**

What does the phrase "hung his head" suggest about Nord?

Ⓐ   He is frightened.

Ⓑ   He is disappointed.

Ⓒ   He is freezing.

Ⓓ   He is famished.

2   How does Nord feel about having lost all communication?

Ⓐ   Puzzled

Ⓑ   Delighted

Ⓒ   Calm

Ⓓ   Lonesome

3   What is the most likely setting of the passage?

Ⓐ   The Arctic

Ⓑ   The Sahara Desert

Ⓒ   The Amazon rainforest

Ⓓ   The Florida wetlands

Reading Workbook

STAAR Reading

Set 7

Instructions

Read each passage. Each passage is followed by three questions.

Read each question carefully. Then select the best answer. Fill in the circle for the correct answer.

Black, Red, and Gold

The modern flag of Germany is a tricolor flag consisting of three horizontal bands of equal size colored black, red, and gold. The flag first appeared in the early 19th century. It was originally used by the Frankfurt Parliament and achieved prominence during the 1848 revolution of the German states. During Nazi Germany, the flag's colors were changed to black, white, and red. The flag was restored after World War II. It has been Germany's national flag since 1949.

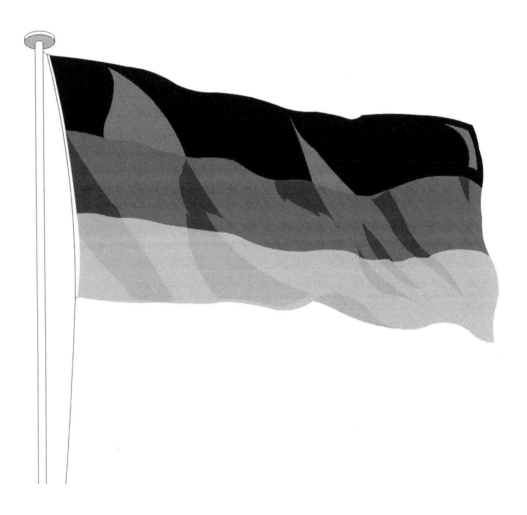

1   Read this sentence from the passage.

> **It was originally used by the Frankfurt Parliament and achieved prominence during the 1848 revolution of the German states.**

What does the phrase "achieved prominence" mean?

Ⓐ   Achieved a win

Ⓑ   Became well-known

Ⓒ   Won an election

Ⓓ   Completed a goal

2   How was the flag changed during Nazi Germany?

Ⓐ   The gold was removed from the flag.

Ⓑ   The stripes were made smaller.

Ⓒ   The number of stripes increased to four.

Ⓓ   The direction of the stripes was altered.

3   How is the passage mainly organized?

Ⓐ   A solution to a problem is described.

Ⓑ   Events are described in the order they occurred.

Ⓒ   Facts are given to support an argument.

Ⓓ   An event in the past is compared to an event today.

Troy McClure

Troy McClure is a reoccurring character in the popular television animation *The Simpsons*. The character was originally based on B-movie actors Troy Donahue and Doug McClure. Troy McClure was voiced by Phil Hartman, who died in 1998. Hartman's death led to the character being retired.

Troy McClure made his final appearance in the tenth season episode titled "Bart the Mother." It was a sad loss for a character that was much-loved by fans.

1   Read this sentence from the passage.

> **Troy McClure is a reoccurring character in the popular television animation *The Simpsons*.**

What does the word <u>reoccurring</u> mean?

    Ⓐ   Occurring again

    Ⓑ   No longer occurring

    Ⓒ   Occurring once

    Ⓓ   Occurring annually

2   Who was Troy McClure named after?

    Ⓐ   The creator of *The Simpsons*

    Ⓑ   The person who was his voice

    Ⓒ   Two B-movie actors

    Ⓓ   Two famous cartoonists

3   Why was the character Troy McClure retired?

    Ⓐ   He was no longer useful in the show.

    Ⓑ   The person who provided his voice died.

    Ⓒ   He was taking the focus off the main characters.

    Ⓓ   He had been appearing in the show too often.

The Human Skeleton

Did you know that there are over 206 bones in the adult human skeleton? Newborn babies have over 270 bones. As a newborn baby grows, some of their bones are fused together.

The skeleton performs several very important functions within our body. These include providing a support framework, protecting vital organs, and playing a crucial role in the generation of blood cells. Bones are also a storage site for many of the minerals our bodies need.

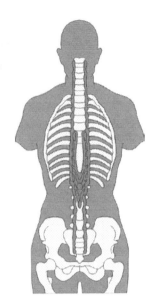

1 Which two words from the passage have about the same meaning?

    Ⓐ   *storage, minerals*

    Ⓑ   *skeleton, bones*

    Ⓒ   *adult, newborn*

    Ⓓ   *vital, crucial*

2 Complete the web below using information from the passage.

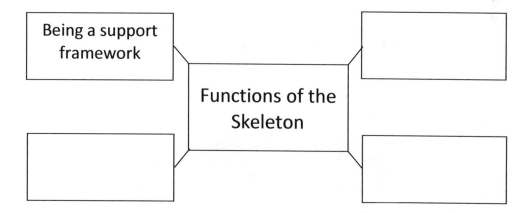

3 According to the passage, how are adults different from children?

    Ⓐ   They have more bones.

    Ⓑ   They have fewer bones.

    Ⓒ   Their bones have more purposes.

    Ⓓ   Their bones have fewer purposes.

The Astronomer

An astronomer used to go out at night to observe the stars. One evening, he was wandering around town with his eyes fixed on the sky. He suddenly tripped and fell into a well. He sat there and groaned about his sores and bruises and cried for help. He pummeled his fists against the well. He looked up and all he could see were the stars. The twinkling stars looked back down on him and laughed.

The astronomer's friend finally heard his cries and made his way over to the well. After hearing the astronomer's story of how he fell, he simply shook his head.

"Old friend, in striving to see into the heavens, you don't manage to see what is on the earth," the friend said.

1   Read this sentence from the passage.

> **One evening, he was wandering around town with his eyes fixed on the sky.**

The word <u>fixed</u> shows that the astronomer was –

Ⓐ   staring

Ⓑ   blinking

Ⓒ   glancing

Ⓓ   glaring

2   Which sentence from the passage contains personification?

Ⓐ   *He sat there and groaned about his sores and bruises and cried for help.*

Ⓑ   *He pummeled his fists against the well.*

Ⓒ   *He looked up and all he could see were the stars.*

Ⓓ   *The twinkling stars looked back down on him and laughed.*

3   The main theme of the passage is about –

Ⓐ   having an interesting hobby

Ⓑ   not being afraid to ask for help

Ⓒ   being careful at all times

Ⓓ   not focusing too much on one thing

Drummer Boy

Tap-tap-tap, ratta-tat-tat. Tim used his two pencils on his school desk like drumsticks. He hummed his favorite tune as he enjoyed daydreaming.

"Tim! Would you cut that out?" Mr. Paulson hollered.

Tim nearly jumped out of his chair as he came back to reality.

"Sorry about that, sir!" Tim said as all the other kids chuckled a little.

Mr. Paulson went back to writing on the board. Tim opened his notebook and wrote in it. *One day I'm going to be in a band*, he wrote.

1 Read this sentence from the passage.

"Tim! Would you cut that out?" Mr. Paulson hollered.

What does the phrase "cut that out" mean?

Ⓐ Scratch it

Ⓑ Remove it

Ⓒ Stop it

Ⓓ Decrease it

2 Which word best describes Tim while he is in class?

Ⓐ Distracted

Ⓑ Anxious

Ⓒ Relaxed

Ⓓ Annoyed

3 Why does the author have text in italics in the last sentence?

Ⓐ To suggest that the text was spoken

Ⓑ To show that it is a flashback

Ⓒ To emphasize the main point

Ⓓ To indicate written text

Reading Workbook

STAAR Reading

Set 8

Instructions

Read each passage. Each passage is followed by three questions.

Read each question carefully. Then select the best answer. Fill in the circle for the correct answer.

Magnetic North

The compass was invented in ancient China around 247 B.C. It became popular for use in navigation by the 11th century. In those early days, they were often used by sailors and explorers. Today, compasses are still used by sailors. They are also used by people doing activities like hiking or orienteering.

Most compass devices consist of a dial with north, east, south, and west marked on them. The compass has a spinning needle mounted in the middle. The needle is magnetized and aligns itself with the Earth's magnetic field. This results in the compass needle always facing toward the north.

1   According to the passage, what original use of compasses is still a common use today?

ⓐ   Sailing

ⓑ   Exploring

ⓒ   Hiking

ⓓ   Orienteering

2   What does the illustration best show?

ⓐ   How to use a compass

ⓑ   What a compass looks like

ⓒ   What a compass can be used for

ⓓ   When the compass was invented

3   What is the second paragraph mainly about?

ⓐ   How a compass works

ⓑ   How compasses have changed

ⓒ   Common uses of a compass

ⓓ   The invention of the compass

Ruler of Macedon

Alexander the Great is one of the most noteworthy kings of all time. He was king of Macedon in north-eastern Greece in 336 B.C. By the age of 30, Alexander the Great had created one of the largest empires in ancient history. He was responsible for the fall of the Persian king Darius III, among many other grand accomplishments. The tactical achievements of Alexander are still taught throughout the world in military academies today.

1   Read this sentence from the passage.

Alexander the Great is one of the most noteworthy kings of all time.

Which word means about the same as <u>noteworthy</u>?

Ⓐ   Enduring

Ⓑ   Celebrated

Ⓒ   Significant

Ⓓ   Damaging

2   Which detail best shows that Alexander the Great is still appreciated today?

Ⓐ   He was king of Macedon.

Ⓑ   He created one of the largest empires ever.

Ⓒ   He caused the fall of the Persian king Darius III.

Ⓓ   His achievements are taught in military academies.

3   What type of passage is "Ruler of Macedon"?

Ⓐ   Realistic fiction

Ⓑ   Biography

Ⓒ   Historical fiction

Ⓓ   Autobiography

The Dwarf Miner

The dwarf picked up a lump of gold from the ground. He stared at it for a few moments and then bit it sharply between his teeth.

"She sure is gold!" he proclaimed excitedly, before picking up his pickaxe.

The dwarf wandered around in front of the rock wall for a few minutes, before swinging his tool into it. After a few hours of mining, the dwarf had a small bowl full of gleaming golden nuggets. He set off happily for home, whistling all the way there.

1   Read this sentence from the passage.

> **"She sure is gold!" he proclaimed excitedly, before picking up his pickaxe.**

Which word means about the same as <u>proclaimed</u>?

Ⓐ   Declared

Ⓑ   Argued

Ⓒ   Whispered

Ⓓ   Assumed

2   Why did the dwarf most likely bite the gold?

Ⓐ   He was confused.

Ⓑ   He needed to check that it was gold.

Ⓒ   He was hungry.

Ⓓ   He wanted to see how much it was worth.

3   Which set of words from the passage is an example of alliteration?

Ⓐ   *lump of gold*

Ⓑ   *bit it sharply*

Ⓒ   *gleaming golden nuggets*

Ⓓ   *whistling a happy tune*

The Desert Oasis

Serian had walked for days in the desert. He wasn't sure if he would ever see anyone again. Serian was lost. He scuffled across the hot desert sand, waiting for nightfall to ease the sweltering heat. Serian reached the peak of a sand dune. He planted himself on the hot sand and took a few moments to rest. Off in the distance, he saw an oasis filled with plants and a large lake. Serian's eyes glimmered and he smiled for the first time in days as he powered on toward the oasis.

1   Which sentence from the passage creates a mood of hopelessness?

    Ⓐ   *Serian had walked for days in the desert.*

    Ⓑ   *He wasn't sure if he would ever see anyone again.*

    Ⓒ   *He planted himself on the hot sand and took a few moments to rest.*

    Ⓓ   *Off in the distance, he saw an oasis filled with plants and a large lake.*

2   The phrase "powered on" shows that Serian –

    Ⓐ   wandered slowly

    Ⓑ   walked with enthusiasm

    Ⓒ   needed more energy

    Ⓓ   was overheating

3   Why is Serian keen for nightfall to come?

    Ⓐ   So he can finally rest

    Ⓑ   Because it will be cooler

    Ⓒ   Because he might be able to spot lights

    Ⓓ   So he can use the stars to guide him

The Park

April 21

Dear Diary,

Today Mom and I went for a walk in the park after school. The park is such a pretty and peaceful place with all of those trees, flowers, and birds. We saw people having picnics, and some kids rowing boats on the lake. Some people were also feeding bread to the ducks.

We saw one man who was painted in silver paint. He was standing completely still and changing his pose every few minutes. While he was still, he looked exactly like a statue! It was pretty amazing to watch. Mom and I took a photo in front of him. We said goodbye and left some change in his tip jar. What a great afternoon!

Harmanie xo

1   Read this sentence from the passage.

He was standing completely still and changing his pose every few minutes.

Which word means the opposite of <u>still</u>?

Ⓐ   Moving

Ⓑ   Noisy

Ⓒ   Silent

Ⓓ   Motionless

2   Describe two things that Harmanie saw people doing in the park.

Things that Harmanie Saw People Doing in the Park
1)
2)

3   What is the setting of the passage?

Ⓐ   Early morning

Ⓑ   About midday

Ⓒ   Late afternoon

Ⓓ   About midnight

Answer Key

Tracking Student Progress

Use the answer key to score each quiz. After scoring each quiz, record the score in the Score Tracker at the back of the book. Tally the scores to find the total once each set of 5 quizzes is complete.

As the student progresses through the sets, test scores will continue to improve as the students develops reading skills and gains confidence.

STAAR Reading Skills

The STAAR reading test given by the state of Texas tests a specific set of skills. The answer key identifies what skill each question is testing. Use the skill listed with each question to identify areas of weakness. Then target revision and instruction accordingly.

The answer key also includes notes on key reading skills that students will need to understand to master the STAAR reading test. Use the notes to review the questions with students so they gain a full understanding of these key reading skills.

Set 1

Flying High

Question	Answer	Reading Skill
1	C	Identify and use synonyms
2	D	Compare and contrast characters
3	D	Locate facts and details in a passage

King of the Jungle

Question	Answer	Reading Skill
1	B	Identify and use antonyms*
2	A	Identify the tone of a passage*
3	B	Draw conclusions based on information in a passage*

*Key Reading Skill: Antonyms

Antonyms are words that have opposite meanings. In the sentence, the word *steady* means "slowly" so the correct answer is the word that means "quickly." The word *rapid* is the correct answer.

*Key Reading Skill: Tone

The tone of a passage refers to the author's attitude. It is how the author feels about the content of the passage. For example, the tone could be playful, sad, cheerful, or witty. In this case, the tone is serious.

*Key Reading Skill: Drawing Conclusions

This question asks which conclusion is supported by the passage. All of the statements could be correct statements, but only one of the statements has facts and details in the passage that support it. The facts on how long lions live in the wild and in captivity support the statement in answer choice B.

Gone Fishing

Question	Answer	Reading Skill
1	A	Make inferences about characters
2	A	Identify the setting of a passage
3	B	Identify and summarize the theme of a passage

The Capybara

Question	Answer	Reading Skill
1	Beavers, chipmunks, rats, mice, or capybara	Summarize information given in a passage
2	C	Identify and use synonyms
3	C	Identify the author's main purpose

The Dentist

Question	Answer	Reading Skill
1	D	Use context to determine the meaning of words
2	B	Make inferences about characters
3	B	Analyze point of view*

*Key Reading Skill: Point of View

This question is asking about the point of view of the passage. There are three main points of view. They are:

- First person – the story is told by a narrator who is a character in the story. The use of the words *I*, *my*, or *we* indicate a first person point of view. *Example: I went for a hike in the mountains. After a while, my legs began to ache.*

- Second person – the story is told by referring to the reader as "you." *Example: You are hiking in the mountains. After a while, your legs begin to ache.*

- Third person – the story is told by a person outside the story. *Example: Jacky went for a hike in the mountains. After a while, her legs began to ache.*

The story is told by a narrator who refers to herself using the words *I* and *my*, so the passage has a first person point of view. This question is asking how the point of view affects the reader. The first person point of view allows the reader to be told about Becky's thoughts and feelings. It allows the reader to understand how Becky felt about going to the dentist. The other answer choices list things that the reader could tell whether the point of view was first person, second person, or third person.

Set 2

A Quiet Night

Question	Answer	Reading Skill
1	A	Understand and analyze word use
2	C	Identify and analyze the mood of a passage*
3	B	Understand and analyze literary techniques (symbolism)*

*Key Reading Skill: Mood

The mood of a passage is the way the passage makes the reader feel. It is the atmosphere of the passage. The mood of the passage is peaceful.

*Key Reading Skill: Symbolism

Symbolism is the use of a word, image, or object to represent something else. In the passage, the candle burning down is a symbol representing the passing of time.

Hillary Clinton

Question	Answer	Reading Skill
1	D	Use words with multiple meanings*
2	A	Identify different types of texts
3	B	Identify the sequence of events

*Key Reading Skill: Multiple Meanings

Some words have more than one meaning. These words are known as homonyms. All the answer choices are possible meanings for the word *serving*. The correct answer is the one that states the meaning of the word *serving* as it is used in the sentence.

I Have a Dream

Question	Answer	Reading Skill
1	D	Identify and use synonyms
2	A	Identify different types of texts*
3	D	Identify details that support a conclusion

*Key Reading Skill: Identifying Genres (Biography)

A biography is a story of someone's life written by someone other than the person described. This is different to an autobiography, which is the story of someone's life written by that person.

Artistic Creativity

Question	Answer	Reading Skill
1	A	Identify and use antonyms*
2	C	Locate facts and details in a passage
3	A	Identify point of view*

*Key Reading Skill: Antonyms

Antonyms are words that have opposite meanings. In this case, you are looking for the word that means "not bizarre."

*Key Reading Skill: Point of View

This question is asking about the point of view of the passage. There are four possible points of view. They are:

- First person – the story is told by a narrator who is a character in the story. The use of the words *I*, *my*, or *we* indicate a first person point of view. *Example: I went for a hike in the mountains. After a while, my legs began to ache.*

- Second person – the story is told by referring to the reader as "you." *Example: You are hiking in the mountains. After a while, your legs begin to ache.*

- Third person limited – the story is told by a person outside the story. The term *limited* refers to how much knowledge the narrator has. The narrator has knowledge of one character, but does not have knowledge beyond what that one character knows, sees, or does. *Example: Jacky went for a hike in the mountains. After a while, her legs began to ache.*

- Third person omniscient – the story is told by a person outside the story. The term *omniscient* refers to how much knowledge the narrator has. An omniscient narrator knows everything about all characters and has unlimited information. *Example: Jacky went for a hike in the mountains. Like most of the other hikers, her legs began to ache.*

The story is told by a narrator who refers to herself using the words *I* and *my*, so the passage has a first person point of view.

What Caterpillars Do

Question	Answer	Reading Skill
1	D	Identify and analyze the mood of a passage*
2	B	Understand and analyze literary techniques (repetition)*
3	D	Identify the characteristics of poems

*Key Reading Skill: Mood

The mood of a passage is the way the passage makes the reader feel. It is the atmosphere of the passage. The mood of the passage is cheerful.

*Key Reading Skill: Repetition

Repetition is a literary technique where words, phrases, or entire lines are repeated. The poem uses repetition in the first stanza where the first and third lines are repeated except for a change in the last word of the line. The use of the phrases "they don't do much" and "they don't know much" is also an example of repetition. The word *chew* is also repeated in the poem.

Set 3

Be Prepared

Question	Answer	Reading Skill
1	Scouts, 11 to 18 Rover Scouts, over 18	Summarize information given in a passage
2	C	Make predictions based on information in a passage
3	C	Identify and use synonyms

Breaking In

Question	Answer	Reading Skill
1	B	Use context to determine the meaning of words
2	B	Identify the author's main purpose
3	B	Distinguish between fact and opinion*

*Key Reading Skill: Fact and Opinion

A fact is a statement that can be proven to be correct. An opinion is a statement that cannot be proven to be correct. An opinion is what somebody thinks about something. The sentence given in answer choice B is a fact. The other sentences are opinions.

Hide and Seek

Question	Answer	Reading Skill
1	A	Identify and use synonyms
2	D	Understand and analyze literary techniques (simile)*
3	C	Use prior knowledge to draw conclusions

*Key Reading Skill: Simile

A simile compares two things using the words "like" or "as." The phrase "like he had just seen a ghost" is an example of a simile.

Cartoons

Question	Answer	Reading Skill
1	B	Identify the meaning of phrases
2	D	Identify and summarize the main idea
3	A	Identify the main idea

Defeat at Waterloo

Question	Answer	Reading Skill
1	D	Understand and analyze word use
2	B	Make inferences about an author's opinion or viewpoint
3	B	Identify the main idea

Set 4

Flying Scavengers

Question	Answer	Reading Skill
1	D	Locate facts and details in a passage
2	B	Identify different types of texts
3	D	Identify the author's main purpose

Danny's Homework

Question	Answer	Reading Skill
1	D	Understand and analyze literary techniques (personification)*
2	B	Make inferences based on information in a passage
3	A	Draw conclusions about characters

*Key Reading Skill: Personification

Personification is a literary technique where objects are given human qualities, or described as if they are human. The laptop is given human qualities by being described as saying something excitedly. Only a person can say something excitedly, so this is an example of personification.

The Evil Candide

Question	Answer	Reading Skill
1	D	Identify and use synonyms
2	A	Identify and analyze the setting of a passage
3	B	Make predictions based on information in a passage

Radiohead

Question	Answer	Reading Skill
1	B	Identify the purpose of specific information
2	B	Identify how a passage is organized*
3	A	Identify the author's main purpose

*Key Reading Skill: Patterns of Organization

There are several common ways that passages are organized. Students will often be asked to identify how a passage, or a paragraph within a passage, is organized. The common patterns of organization are:

- Cause and effect – a cause of something is described and then its effect is described
- Chronological order, or sequence of events – events are described in the order that they occurred
- Compare and contrast – two or more people, events, places, or objects are compared or contrasted
- Problem and solution – a problem is described and then a solution to the problem is given
- Main idea/supporting details – a main idea is stated and then details are given to support the main idea
- Question and answer – a question is asked and then answered

Belarus

Question	Answer	Reading Skill
1	A	Understand and analyze information shown on maps
2	B	Draw conclusions based on information in a passage
3	C	Identify different types of texts

Set 5

The Dog and the River

Question	Answer	Reading Skill
1	D	Identify different types of texts*
2	B	Identify and summarize the theme of a passage
3	A	Summarize the plot of a passage*

*Key Reading Skill: Identifying Genres (Fable)

A fable is a story that has the main purpose of teaching a moral lesson. Fables usually have animals as characters.

*Key Reading Skill: Summarize

A summary is a description of the main events of the passage. A summary should include all the important events and information, but should not include extra information not included in the passage or an interpretation of the passage.

Many students find it difficult to identify the correct answer in these types of questions because the wrong answers will often also be partially correct. Details on why each answer is correct or incorrect are given below:

Answer choice A is correct because it describes the main events of the passage.

Answer choice B is incorrect because it does not describe all of the events accurately. The dog does not lose the fight, so this information is incorrect.

Answer choice C is incorrect because it includes an interpretation of how the dog feels. This summary does describe most of the events correctly, but the last sentence contains information that is not given in the passage.

Answer choice D is incorrect because it does not include all the important information. It describes some events that occur in the passage, but leaves out that the dog drops the meat because he is trying to get the larger piece of meat.

This is important to the plot and theme of the passage, and so should be included in the summary.

Bananas

Question	Answer	Reading Skill
1	B	Identify the meaning of phrases
2	B	Identify the sequence of events
3	C	Make inferences about characters

Brain in a Bottle

Question	Answer	Reading Skill
1	D	Use words with multiple meanings*
2	A	Identify the purpose of text features
3	A	Identify the main idea

*Key Reading Skill: Multiple Meanings

Some words have more than one meaning. These words are known as homonyms. All the answer choices are possible meanings for the word *conduct*. The correct answer is the one that states the meaning of the word *conduct* as it is used in the sentence.

Antique Map

Question	Answer	Reading Skill
1	C	Identify the purpose of specific information
2	B	Understand written directions
3	D	Use prior knowledge to draw conclusions

A Special Student

Question	Answer	Reading Skill
1	D	Identify point of view*
2	C	Identify the sequence of events
3	D	Understand and interpret information given in a passage

*Key Reading Skill: Point of View

This question is asking about the point of view of the passage. There are four possible points of view. They are:

- First person – the story is told by a narrator who is a character in the story. The use of the words *I*, *my*, or *we* indicate a first person point of view. *Example: I went for a hike in the mountains. After a while, my legs began to ache.*

- Second person – the story is told by referring to the reader as "you." This point of view is rarely used. *Example: You are hiking in the mountains. After a while, your legs begin to ache.*

- Third person limited – the story is told by a person outside the story. The term *limited* refers to how much knowledge the narrator has. The narrator has knowledge of one character, but does not have knowledge beyond what that one character knows, sees, or does. *Example: Jacky went for a hike in the mountains. After a while, her legs began to ache.*

- Third person omniscient – the story is told by a person outside the story. The term *omniscient* refers to how much knowledge the narrator has. An omniscient narrator knows everything about all characters and has unlimited information. *Example: Jacky went for a hike in the mountains. Like most of the other hikers, her legs began to ache.*

The story is told by a person outside the story, so the passage has a third person point of view. The narrator is omniscient because he or she describes the thoughts and feelings of June and the school children.

Set 6

Photosynthesis

Question	Answer	Reading Skill
1	C	Identify and use antonyms*
2	D	Identify the author's main purpose
3	C	Locate facts and details in a passage

*Key Reading Skill: Antonyms

Antonyms are words that have opposite meanings. The words *absorbed* and *released* have opposite meanings.

The Little Things

Question	Answer	Reading Skill
1	D	Identify and analyze the mood of a passage*
2	D	Draw conclusions about characters
3	A	Identify and summarize the theme of a passage

*Key Reading Skill: Mood

The mood of a passage is the way the passage makes the reader feel. It is the atmosphere of the passage. The phrase "strolled out to his garden" creates a feeling of calm.

Sweet Tooth

Question	Answer	Reading Skill
1	A	Use context to determine the meaning of words
2	A	Identify the purpose of text features
3	C	Draw conclusions based on information in a passage

The Stanley Cup

Question	Answer	Reading Skill
1	A	Identify and use synonyms
2	C	Identify the purpose of specific information
3	B	Distinguish between fact and opinion*

*Key Reading Skill: Fact and Opinion

A fact is a statement that can be proven to be correct. An opinion is a statement that cannot be proven to be correct. An opinion is what somebody thinks about something. The sentence given in answer choice B is an opinion. It describes what the author thinks and cannot be proven to be true.

Snowed In

Question	Answer	Reading Skill
1	B	Make inferences based on information in a passage
2	C	Draw conclusions about characters
3	A	Identify the setting of a passage

Set 7

Black, Red, and Gold

Question	Answer	Reading Skill
1	B	Identify the meaning of phrases
2	A	Locate facts and details in a passage
3	B	Identify how a passage is organized*

*Key Reading Skill: Patterns of Organization

There are several common ways that passages are organized. Students will often be asked to identify how a passage, or a paragraph within a passage, is organized. The common patterns of organization are:

- Cause and effect – a cause of something is described and then its effect is described
- Chronological order, or sequence of events – events are described in the order that they occurred
- Compare and contrast – two or more people, events, places, or objects are compared or contrasted
- Problem and solution – a problem is described and then a solution to the problem is given
- Main idea/supporting details – a main idea is stated and then details are given to support the main idea
- Question and answer – a question is asked and then answered

Troy McClure

Question	Answer	Reading Skill
1	A	Use prefixes and suffixes to determine the meaning of a word*
2	C	Locate facts and details in a passage
3	B	Understand cause and effect

*Key Reading Skill: Prefixes and Suffixes

A prefix is a word part that is placed at the start of a word, such as *un-* or *dis-*. A suffix is a word part that is placed at the end of a word, such as *-less* or *-ly*. The word *reoccurring* is the base word *occurring* with the prefix *re-* added to the start. The word *reoccurring* means "occurring again."

The Human Skeleton

Question	Answer	Reading Skill
1	D	Identify and use synonyms
2	Protecting vital organs Generating blood cells Storing minerals	Summarize information given in a passage
3	B	Compare and contrast two items

The Astronomer

Question	Answer	Reading Skill
1	A	Understand and analyze word use
2	D	Understand and analyze literary techniques (personification)*
3	D	Identify and summarize the theme of a passage

*Key Reading Skill: Personification

Personification is a literary technique where objects are given human qualities, or described as if they are human. The stars are given human qualities by being described as looking down and laughing. Stars cannot actually look or laugh, so this is an example of personification.

Drummer Boy

Question	Answer	Reading Skill
1	C	Identify the meaning of phrases
2	A	Draw conclusions about characters
3	D	Identify the purpose of text features

Set 8

Magnetic North

Question	Answer	Reading Skill
1	A	Locate facts and details in a passage
2	B	Understand and analyze illustrations and photographs
3	A	Identify the main idea

Ruler of Macedon

Question	Answer	Reading Skill
1	C	Identify and use synonyms
2	D	Identify details that support a conclusion
3	B	Identify different types of texts*

*Key Reading Skill: Identifying Genres (Biography)

A biography is a story of someone's life written by someone other than the person described. This is different to an autobiography, which is the story of someone's life written by that person.

The Dwarf Miner

Question	Answer	Reading Skill
1	A	Identify and use synonyms
2	B	Make inferences based on information in a passage
3	C	Understand and analyze literary techniques (alliteration)*

*Key Reading Skill: Alliteration

Alliteration is a literary technique where consonant sounds are repeated in neighboring words. The phrase "gleaming golden nuggets" uses alliteration because of the repeated "g" sound.

The Desert Oasis

Question	Answer	Reading Skill
1	B	Identify and analyze the mood of a passage*
2	B	Understand and analyze word use
3	B	Locate facts and details in a passage

*Key Reading Skill: Mood

The mood of a passage is the way the passage makes the reader feel. It is the atmosphere of the passage. The sentence in answer choice B creates a mood of hopelessness.

The Park

Question	Answer	Reading Skill
1	A	Identify and use antonyms*
2	Having picnics, rowing boats, or feeding ducks	Summarize information given in a passage
3	C	Identify the setting of a passage

*Key Reading Skill: Antonyms

Antonyms are words that have opposite meanings. In this case, you are looking for the word that means "not still."

Score Tracker

Set 1

Flying High	/3
Gone Fishing	/3
King of the Jungle	/3
The Capybara	/3
The Dentist	/3
Total	**/15**

Set 3

Be Prepared	/3
Breaking In	/3
Hide and Seek	/3
Cartoons	/3
Defeat at Waterloo	/3
Total	**/15**

Set 2

A Quiet Night	/3
Hillary Clinton	/3
I Have a Dream	/3
Artistic Creativity	/3
What Caterpillars Do	/3
Total	**/15**

Set 4

Flying Scavengers	/3
Danny's Homework	/3
The Evil Candide	/3
Radiohead	/3
Belarus	/3
Total	**/15**

Score Tracker

Set 5

The Dog and the River	/3
Bananas	/3
Brain in a Bottle	/3
Antique Map	/3
A Special Student	/3
Total	**/15**

Set 7

Black, Red, and Gold	/3
Troy McClure	/3
The Human Skeleton	/3
The Astronomer	/3
Drummer Boy	/3
Total	**/15**

Set 6

Photosynthesis	/3
The Little Things	/3
Sweet Tooth	/3
The Stanley Cup	/3
Snowed In	/3
Total	**/15**

Set 8

Magnetic North	/3
Ruler of Macedon	/3
The Dwarf Miner	/3
The Desert Oasis	/3
The Park	/3
Total	**/15**

Texas Test Prep Practice Test Book

For additional reading test prep, get the Texas Test Prep Practice Test Book. It contains 8 reading mini-tests, focused vocabulary quizzes, plus a full-length STAAR Reading practice test.

Texas Test Prep Math

Help with the Texas STAAR tests is also available for math!

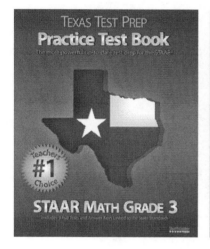 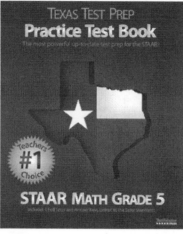 

- Powerful up-to-date test prep for the STAAR Math test
- Practice Test Book and Student Quiz Book available
- Covers every math skill needed by Texas students
- Books available from Grades 3 through to 8

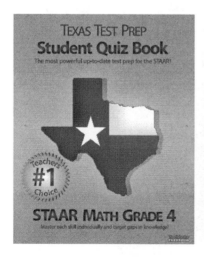 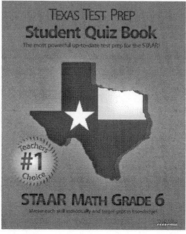 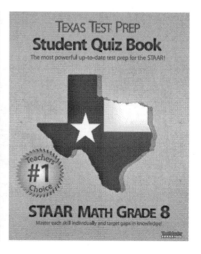